MW00365968

The Little
Book of
Forgiveness

For Christine, who taught me
why forgiveness matters.

The Little
Book of
Forgiveness

Kitty Guilsborough

An Hachette UK Company

www.hachette.co.uk

First published in Great Britain in 2021 by Gaia, an imprint of
Octopus Publishing Group Ltd
Carmelite House
50 Victoria Embankment
London EC4Y 0DZ

www.octopusbooks.co.uk

Distributed in the US by Hachette Book Group
1290 Avenue of the Americas
4th and 5th Floors
New York, NY 10104

Distributed in Canada by
Canadian Manda Group
664 Annette St.
Toronto, Ontario,
Canada M6S 2C8

ISBN 978-1-85675-442-2

A CIP catalogue record for this book is available from
the British Library.

Printed and bound in China

10 9 8 7 6 5 4 3 2 1

Commissioning Editor: Natalie Bradley
Assistant Editor: Sarah Kyle
Art Director: Juliette Norsworthy
Production Controller: Serena Savini
Copy Editor: Clare Churly
Proofreader: Jane Birch
Design and illustration: Abi Read

Contents

Introduction

Nobody picks up a book about forgiveness unless they've
been wronged.

Somebody hurt you. Somebody hurt you badly enough
that you couldn't just forget it. Somebody did something
to you – or someone you love – that was so huge, so
heartbreaking, so completely devastating that you're
still thinking about it today.

There are thousands of books you could have chosen to read right now. There are hundreds of other things you could be doing. There's a whole world out there waiting for you. But you're here, reading this book, and you're still thinking about the hurtful thing that happened. And yet you're also thinking – perhaps for the first time, or perhaps for the thousandth time – about how you can heal.

Something in you wants to move on from this pain. You no longer wish to be defined by it. I know this because you picked up this book. You didn't pick up *The Little Book of Blame*. You aren't here for *The Little Book of Revenge* or *The Little Book of Retribution*. This isn't *The Little Book of Punishment*. This isn't even *The Little Book of Justice*. This book is about forgiveness.

It's hard to define the concept of forgiveness, partly because it means different things to different people and partly because it's always difficult to define an absence. Forgiveness is a progress *toward* an absence of feeling: an absence of anger, an absence of resentment, an absence of a desire toward revenge. Forgiveness is a deliberate, conscious decision to relinquish feelings of resentment or anger toward a person who has wronged you. It's a letting go, a moving forward, a decision to choose the future instead of dwelling on the past. It's about choosing *now* instead of *then*. It's about living where you *are* instead of where you *were*. It's about choosing any one of the thousands of other tales you could share about yourself, instead of focusing on this one story about your pain. It's about changing the narrative. It's about seeing yourself as a *survivor* instead of a *victim*. It's about being in control of the narrative. It's about taking charge of your own story.

Because here's the real thing about forgiveness: it's all about you.

This is a book about you.

The Process of Forgiveness

Before we begin, I want to say that I'm so sorry something hurtful happened to you. I don't know what it was that happened, of course, but I do know it was wrong. Someone behaved to you in a way that wasn't just. Someone treated you unkindly and unfairly, and they hurt you.

We're all showing up to this book with trauma. We're all here – you, me and everyone else holding this book in their hands, the pages pressing into our fingers in the same way they're pressing into yours – with our own private grief. I don't know what your trauma is, but I do know it was wrong. It was wrong and it shouldn't have happened.

Perhaps nobody has ever told you how sorry they are. Perhaps you've never told anyone what happened because you don't want anyone to feel sorry for you. Well, I don't feel sorry for you. I'm just sorry that something happened to you that hurt. I'm sorry that something happened to you that you're here to try to forgive.

This process isn't going to be easy. Real forgiveness never is. It wants us to look deep inside ourselves, and then out again at the world that's waiting for us. It wants us to reckon with what was done to us – and what we've done to ourselves. It wants us to understand our own pain and our own culpability, to relive the wrong that was done to us and to work out why it was done in the first place. Real forgiveness requires compassion: for ourselves, for others and for the people who hurt us. It calls for empathy and communication and perspective. It needs love.

I think you can forgive. And I'll do it too: a double whammy.
This is a team effort. It's a team exercise in the kind of
profound love that will change your life for the better.
I believe in you. I believe, essentially, in the best of you, and
that's the theme of this book. We're going to believe the best
of people, we're going to trust them and we're going to trust
them to manage themselves as we manage
ourselves. We're going to learn to take
responsibility only for ourselves and carry
the burdens – and joys – of our own
choices. We're going to do the only thing
we can do, which is love ourselves the
best way we can.

I'm so glad and proud that you're here.
I love you. Let's do this. Let's turn the
page and get stuck in.

Why Forgive?

How do we do it? How do we forgive someone? And more importantly, why should we forgive them? We're the ones who've been wronged. We're the ones who've been hurt. Why is it on us to do anything more? Why is this our problem to solve?

Unluckily for us, forgiveness isn't about the person who hurt us, not really. (They can't make things better. They did the hurtful thing, and in some cases continue to do it.) No one else can help us move past this pain, which is why forgiveness has to be our job. To paraphrase Maya Angelou, the greatest gift you can give yourself is forgiveness. Let's give ourselves this gift.

We know we need to forgive to move forward. But why should we *want* to move forward? Why should we want to trip merrily into the future if we don't feel justice has been served? Why should it be on us to *get over* the harm that was done? Well, those are good questions. You're allowed to feel like this. You don't have to skim over the injustice. It doesn't make you a bad person for feeling this way.

You might feel a kind of societal and social pressure to forgive, as if you're making everything worse by being stuck in your own trauma. There are many stories of victims forgiving attackers, grieving families forgiving terrorists, women forgiving their violent partners, and these stories are often held up as inspirational. And of course they are. But when you're not *there*, when you're not feeling it, when the world feels against you, this kind of radical forgiveness can feel so distant as to be impossible. It can feel like you're somehow a lesser person for not being able to move on like those magical heroes of forgiveness. It can feel like an insult.

However, this book isn't about other people and the challenges they faced, it's about *you*: your life and your feelings. It's about meeting you where you are, right now, trying to forgive.

Real Forgiveness

People often seem to think of forgiveness as a quick fix: an easy solution to a huge and complicated problem. Tales of bereaved parents who have forgiven their children's killers, for instance, often make headlines, the stories seeming to suggest that the act of forgiveness means the pain is finished and the world can now move on. Thinking of forgiveness like this can be problematic, particularly when such examples are used as weapons to encourage us to forgive: they moved on, so why can't you? Don't you want to do the right thing? Just accept the apology; smile and nod, then go home and cry in private where nobody else can see.

This is *all wrong*. There is no healing in this kind of coerced forgiveness, no real forgiveness in it at all, and certainly no love. So what is real forgiveness? How do we do it properly? And why?

There's no adequate synonym for the word 'forgiveness', not really. To forgive isn't to pardon or excuse or apologize. Forgiveness isn't the same as an acquittal or absolution. The thesaurus suggests the phrases 'kiss and make up' and 'turn the other cheek' as possible substitutions, but neither really cuts it. Forgiveness isn't about kissing, or even making up. It's not about turning the other cheek passively. It's not about letting people hurt you again. Forgiveness is only itself, and perhaps it's best defined as a letting go of something: letting go of anger, letting go of resentment, letting go of revenge.

Understanding Resentment

Resentment, as Nelson Mandela famously said, is like 'drinking poison and then hoping it will kill your enemies'. This isn't just a metaphor, it's physiologically and biologically true. Resentment destroys us physically, mentally and socially. It can consume our whole lives from within. Holding onto resentment damages only ourselves. This isn't to say there aren't certain benefits to resentment. Pain, resentment and suffering all have a purpose in our lives: they shape us, drive us and make us. And yet, in the long term, they can cause serious damage. Studies have shown that holding onto resentment makes us far more likely to suffer from depression and anxiety. Resentment can make us unhappy, tense and stressed.

There is almost no element of your physical wellbeing that doesn't depend on your mental wellbeing. The body and the brain are so intimately linked that what damages one damages the other. This makes complete sense, right? We get headaches when we're working too hard and we clench our jaw when we're angry, but it goes further than that. Stress makes us vulnerable to all kinds of problems, from heart disease to diabetes. Stress makes us more likely to have high blood pressure, and more likely to be obese, both of which in turn make us more vulnerable to things such as viruses, bacteria and cell mutations.

The Symptoms of Stress

Medical establishments, from the NHS in the UK to the Mayo Clinic in the US, agree that the following are all symptoms of stress:

- Headaches or dizziness

- Muscle tension or pain

- Stomach problems

- Chest pain or a faster heartbeat

- Sexual problems

- Difficulty concentrating

- Struggling to make decisions

- Feeling overwhelmed

- Constantly worrying

- Being forgetful

- Being irritable and snappy

- Sleeping too much or too little

- Eating too much or too little

- Avoiding certain places or people

- Drinking or smoking more

Furthermore, stress reduces our ability to take action against these problems. If we're stressed, we're less likely to exercise, eat right and participate in activities like meditation. We smoke more, drink more and sleep less. We lose friends and family to our moods. We destroy our own support network from the inside out. All of which leads to us feel even more stressed and cope even less well; it's a vicious cycle, and it just keeps getting worse and worse every time we go round.

The Effects of Stress

Stress increases our levels of cortisol and adrenaline. Raised long-term, cortisol and adrenaline can cause serious problems in the body: too much cortisol damages our ability to learn and process information, lowers our resistance to infection and reduces our ability to handle infection once it happens, which makes us more likely to get sick and less likely to get better.

Carolyn Aldwin, the director of the Center for Healthy Aging Research at Oregon State University, USA, ran a study that followed 1,293 men for a number of years. 'People who always perceived their daily life to be over-the-top stressful were three times more likely to die over the period of study than people who rolled with the punches

and didn't find daily life very stressful,' Aldwin told America's National Public Radio (NPR) in 2014.[1] The American Medical Association claims that 'stress is the basic cause for more than 60 per cent of all human illnesses and diseases'.[2] And look: a major cause of stress is – you guessed it – resentment. Holding onto resentment is literally killing us.

We have to forgive so that we can move on. We have to make things right, not for the perpetrator, but for our own health and wellbeing. We have to forgive so that the pain caused by our trauma isn't magnified, and so that we don't take the hurt that was done to us, and keep hurting ourselves, over and over again. We don't want to take that hurt and place it on our own friends and family. We have to forgive, not for the perpetrator but for the people we love.

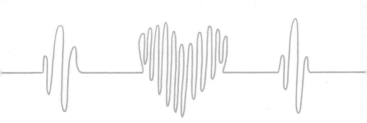

Five Steps to Forgiveness

Over the next five chapters, we're going
to look at five steps to forgiveness.
They are:

1 Acceptance

2 Empathy

3 Acknowledgment

4 Meaning

5 Perspective and Gratitude

Each step in the process is necessary, and
should be followed in order, but feel free to
spend as long as you like on each stage. Some of
these steps won't be easy. Some of them will hurt you
more before you heal, just like a doctor might have to reset
a broken bone or clean a wound with saline and alcohol to
start the healing process.

We can't forgive without understanding *who* we're forgiving and *what* we're forgiving them for. We can't forgive without trying to understand why this wrong happened to us and what it meant – and means – for our lives. Examining these things is brave, hard, good and, above all, necessary. We have to be able to tell a different story about our lives: a bigger, more beautiful story. We need to become the main character – the hero, the narrator – of our own story.

1

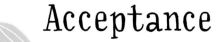

Acceptance

We cannot forgive trauma without accepting trauma.

We have to understand *what* happened to us. We need to accept that something was taken from us. What was taken might be as specific as an *object*, as nebulous as a sense of *identity* or as all-pervasive as *time*. Something has been lost, and it cannot be restored.

To forgive the loss, we have to accept the loss. To accept the loss, we have to understand the loss. How can we change the story if we don't understand the story to begin with?

Too often we try to forgive before we really know what we're forgiving or understand the harm that's been done. This gets us nowhere. In fact, this often leads to more resentment, more suffering and more harm. If we feel compelled to forgive without understanding what or why we're forgiving, we just create extra stress in the body.

Think of it this way: just as a doctor needs to diagnose the illness before they can decide on a course of treatment, so we need to understand the sources of our pain before we know best how to manage it.

Where Are You?

It's not enough just to know how we got here, we need to know where *here* actually is.

Picture yourself lost on a moor. The rain beats down around you. The wind howls. There are paths leading in several directions, some more worn than others. There are also other options: walls you could climb, trees you could hide under, maybe even a barn where you could shelter.

In your freezing hands you're holding a soggy map. You know where you started your journey, sure. You know where you were when you left home. But where are you now? Every twist and turn you've taken has brought you a step further into the unknown. How can the map help you if you don't know your location? How can you move forward?

This chapter is about finding where you are on the map. It is about learning to read the landmarks of your own trauma in order to put your finger down and say, clearly and simply, 'Here I am'.

We're not going to try to solve anything in this chapter. Right here, right now, you're free from the pressure of sorting this out. You don't have to be better. You don't have to be fixed. You're under no obligation, here, to be the bigger person, though we'll get to that later, don't you worry.

Accepting Your Pain

This is a place for pain. It's a place for *your* pain, just as it is: big, small, petty or profound. Bring your pain here, and let's look at it.

There's this impulse, sometimes, to sweep pain under the carpet. We think that if we're not looking at the pain it's gone away, as if the pain will simply dissipate into the mist if nobody acknowledges it. I can't be hurting! Look, I'm smiling! I'm fine!

You're smiling. Maybe you've brushed your hair, uploaded a picture to social media and turned up to work today. Maybe you do that every day. Maybe you make the best of your situation. Maybe you never talk about your pain. Maybe this rings a bell with you. Maybe there's part of you that thinks, 'I've been doing that for years!' And you know what? If that's the case that's *amazing*. I mean it. Hiding your pain got you here, didn't it? It's kept you going. You managed.

You put the pain in a box, shoved the box on a shelf and shut the door tight. And yet somehow, here we are. You picked up this book – or someone gave it to you – and you're still reading. You're still here, looking for a way to forgive, because the thing in that box is howling and yelling and it won't shut up. You can hear it despite all the locks and bolts and soundproofing your clever mind has created to protect you. You're still here, because the pain's still here. You're *still hurting.*

Remember the pressures of pain that we talked about in the Introduction (see page 14)? You might be being made to feel that your pain is someone else's problem. But you know what? Forget that. Your pain is real, your pain is legitimate and you get to feel it. You get to feel it for as long as you want, but only as long as you want.

Pain is helpful. Pain is a warning. Pain can be important.

Making Time for This Process

On the following pages is one of my favourite exercises,
inspired by a mindfulness exercise known as a body scan.
I tend to do it at the beginning of any therapeutic work.

This exercise will help us draw a line between the day that's
been and the time we're about to spend together as we work
through the rest of this chapter. We're going to need some
time alone, somewhere we won't be disturbed, so that we
can go deep into our past and our trauma. I can't tell you this
process is going to be easy, or even very fun, but it will be
useful. We're going to use our pain to put ourselves back
on the map.

But before we do that, let's start by making time for that
mindfulness exercise.

Body Scan (I)

Find a place where you won't be disturbed. It needs to be somewhere you can stay for 20 minutes (or maybe a little more), somewhere peaceful and somewhere safe. Thank you for trusting me with this.

Sit or lie down comfortably, close your eyes and breathe out. *Really* breathe out: breathe out every scrap of stale air that's languishing down in the bottom of your lungs, every particle. Breathe out everything that the day has brought you and then breathe in just as deeply. Inhale. Taste the air on your tongue and in your throat. Feel the air filling your lungs. Breathe in and then out again.

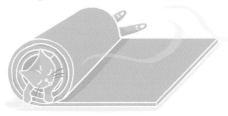

This time, I want you to breathe out the specifics of your day. What's bothering you? What's nagging at you? What's frustrated you this morning? Breathe in (deeper than that, as deep as you can) and then out again. What have you brought with you to this exercise? What have you brought to this room? Breathe in and out. Is this exercise hard? Are you stressed? Are you in pain?

Breathe in, and out again. On the next inhale, I want you to imagine bringing the air right down to your toes (however that looks like to you). Feel the air move through your entire body: the spine, the belly, the hips, the legs, the four corners of the feet. Feel your toes. Feel every toe on each foot. Do your toes hurt? Maybe you've never had to contemplate your toes before. Breathe into each toe (whatever that means to you). Breathe for the little toes, the middle toes, the big toes. Do they hurt? Where are they hurting? Breathe in and then breathe the pain out. Picture it, if you can.

Breathe for the balls of your feet, the soles of your feet, the tops of your feet. Is there tension there? Do they hurt? Do you hurt? Breathe in and then breathe the pain out.

Breathe for your ankles, your shins, your calves, your knees. Any pain? Any tension? Breathe in and then breathe the pain out.

Breathe for your thighs, hips and pelvis. Bring your attention and your breath right down into the bones, the muscles, the organs and the blood. Any pain? Any tension? Any feelings or sensations? How do you feel? Breathe in and then breathe the pain out.

Move your attention up your spine and into your rib cage, your lower back, your upper back, your belly, your chest and your shoulders. Any pain? Any sensation? Breathe in and then breathe the pain out. Now focus on your arms, elbows, hands and fingers, including your fingertips, palms and wrists. Let your attention run along the lines of the bones, and then back up into your shoulders, the top of your spine and the base of your neck. Is there tension there? Is there pain? Is there any sensation to notice? Notice everything. You are worth consideration. Your pain and sensations are worth considering. You must take your pain into account when you work out where to go, and how to do it. You have to acknowledge and accept your pain. Breathe in and then breathe the pain out. I see you.

Now move your attention to your head and your face: the jaw, the cheeks, the temples. Are you clenching your jaw? Are you holding your face rigid? Relax your face; relax as far as you can. Breathe in and then breathe the pain out.

What's hurting? What's helping? Where are you carrying tension? Give yourself permission to answer honestly. You don't need to put on a brave face here. You don't need to say it's nothing. Be yourself, as absolutely as you can. The most helpful thing you can do is to tell yourself the truth. What hurts? Why are you here? What do you need?

When you open your eyes, be proud of yourself. It isn't easy to look at your own pain like that, and it isn't easy to sit or lie like that. It's difficult to find the time without being put off by internal allegations of self-indulgence or dangerous decadence. This isn't an indulgent exercise; it's necessary for your own wellbeing and that of the people around you. You need to know. You have to *know*.

Telling the Story

The first step to forgiveness is to acknowledge our pain. We need to make space for our pain and our sorrow. We need to appropriately understand the ways we've been damaged and the effects this damage has had on our lives. We need to be allowed the space to say, 'Here is what happened to me. Here is my story.'

You know the story. This is the story you tell yourself whenever you think about your pain or about what it is you've come here to forgive. Tell me your story.

Writing can be enormously useful, therapeutically. Many scientists have shown that writing about our pain decreases instances of depression and anxiety. In fact, writing acts as an excellent therapeutic tool for many psychological and mental disorders. A 2005 study from the UK's Royal College of Psychiatrists,[3] published by the Cambridge University Press, declared, 'participants are asked to write about [traumatic] events for 15–20 minutes on 3–5 occasions. Those who do so generally have significantly better physical and psychological outcomes compared with those who write about neutral topics.'

Furthermore, expressive writing, like keeping a journal, is scientifically linked to better physical health, particularly if writing about trauma. Being able to express our emotions has a tangible link to feeling, generally, *better*: better immune function, for instance, lower blood pressure and better recovery times. It has even been linked to better wound healing. In a 2013 study at New Zealand's University of

Auckland,[4] participants were asked to write about their thoughts and feelings for three consecutive days and were then given a (medically necessary!) biopsy. The study then observed the participants' rate of healing: 11 days later, 76 per cent of the writers were fully healed, in contrast to only 42 per cent of the control group. 'We think writing about distressing events helped participants make sense of the events and reduce distress,' one of the scholars explained to *Scientific American*.

So let's write. Let's write the story.

What Happened? (I)

For this exercise, you're going to need a new notebook and a pen, or at least, a new word-processing document. This is your Forgiveness Journal. We'll be working in it through each chapter of this book, using it as a safe space to process our most difficult feelings. This journal is private, it's sacred and it's just for you. Nobody else gets to read it. You can be yourself here, as vulnerable and angry and flawed as you like.

Turn to a blank page, a dedicated blank page just for you and your story, and tell me what happened.

If you're finding this hard, start with the name of the person who hurt you. If you don't know the name of the person, start with a description. Who hurt you? A single sentence.

What did they do? A single sentence.

When? A sentence.

Where? A sentence.

How did they make you *feel*? A sentence.

Now go back and expand on those sentences. Expand each section, giving yourself room to feel. Be melodramatic! Be self-indulgent! Be as descriptive as you can, without hurting yourself further. What happened? What happened next? What happened after that? And so on.

As the Greater Good Science Center at the University of California, Berkeley, USA, recommends, 'Reflect on the psychological and physical harm [the person's offense] may have caused. Consider how your views of humanity and trust of others may have changed as a result of this offense.'

Nobody else is going to see this, remember. This isn't an official statement. Nobody is going to fact check any of this. Say how it felt, what you saw and what you remember. I will believe you without asking a single question. You don't have to prove anything. Just bring your pain, bring your story and bring your trauma. Tell me what happened, and how it was.

Well done. You've been incredibly brave. Stay here as long as you need to, then let's turn the page together.

2

Empathy

According to a 2003 study at Virginia Commonwealth University, Richmond, Virginia, USA,[5] there are two types of forgiveness: decisional and emotional.

Decisional forgiveness means deciding on a conscious level to behave toward the transgressor as you did before the hurtful event, acting in all ways as if the incident never happened. It's a series of deliberate, intellectual, ongoing choices. It means that the person who hurt you is 'released from the debt', as the psychologists put it. 'Granting decisional forgiveness might change negative motivations but not change negative emotions,' says the study. 'Some people grant forgiveness and sincerely never intend to seek revenge or avoid the offender, yet they remain bitter, resentful, hostile, hateful, angry, and fearful toward the offender.'

What this means is we can decide to forgive, we can choose to move on, and yet, unless we really feel it, we'll still suffer the detrimental effects of 'unforgiveness'. We need to have emotional forgiveness, too, and emotional forgiveness is the hard part. Emotional forgiveness comes from love. Unconditional love, according to the study.

Unconditional Love

I know. *I know.* We just spent a full chapter thinking about how we were hurt, the ways we were let down and the ways we were damaged. We established all the ways the perpetrator changed the course of our lives — and now we need to *love* them? That's crazy!

It's probably impossible for you to imagine loving the person who hurt you. That's fine. It makes total sense. However, what we're going to do in this chapter is try to love them anyway. You're not going to like it. But I promise, it will help.

First, let's unpack this idea of unconditional love a bit. I don't mean you need to love the person directly, at least not exclusively. You don't have to make them your best friend. You don't need to speak to them ever again if you don't want to. This person can be gone from your life. And yet, we're going to try to love them because, as the Virginia Commonwealth University study says, 'experiences of positive emotions such as empathy, sympathy, compassion, or love... systematically neutralize the stressfulness of unforgiveness and promote forgiveness'.

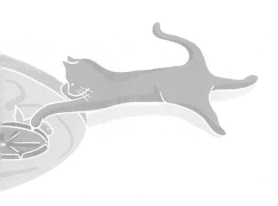

Positive emotions actively work against the stress we feel and cultivating these feelings will actively *help* our recovery. So we're going to try to love the person, and understand them, and (oh no!) even empathize with them. We're going to try to understand why they did what they did.

Pain is complicated. Perhaps the simple story we've been telling ourselves is messier and more complex than we've been admitting. Or maybe it isn't; maybe the person who hurt us is one of the few true villains in the world!

Maybe we'll get to the end of this chapter and nothing will have changed. Whatever the case, it's worth trying to love the person because we need the emotional forgiveness that comes from unconditional love.

The Injustice Gap

Let's get technical for a moment: let's talk about what psychologists call 'the injustice gap'. The 'injustice gap' is, according to a 2015 study published in the *Psychology of Religion and Spirituality*,[6] 'the degree to which victims perceive the aftermath of an offense as not meeting expectations of ideal justice. The magnitude of the injustice gap has been hypothesized to be proportional to the difficulty of forgiving an offence'.

Okay, what does this mean? Basically, the injustice gap is the gulf between what happened to you and what happened to the other person. This discrepancy is the hardest thing to accept. It's the thing that stands between your personhood and theirs. You suffered, so why didn't they?

If you feel you suffered a lot while they suffered not at all, it's hard to forgive. If you suffered only a tiny bit and they suffered greatly, it's easy to forgive. This is pretty logical, right? It makes sense. People like things to be fair. Even little children understand that we need things to feel equal in order to move on. That's why perceptions of justice are so important. That's why, psychologically, we want the

perpetrators to be punished. That's why victims can start to move on after a trial, after the person who hurt them is themself suffering.

Justice evens out our pain and allows us to move on. The smaller the injustice gap, the easier it is to forgive. If we're both in pain – if we're equals – we can get past things. But as we've already covered, this isn't *The Little Book of Justice*. We know we don't have the power to mete out punishment, and we don't actually want to hurt other people ourselves. So how can we decrease our perception of the injustice gap? How can we make that gap as small and easy to cross as possible? And what does all this have to do with unconditional love?

Empathy for the Person Who Hurt You

For this exercise you will need your Forgiveness Journal (see page 41). You need a new page – a blank page – and you also need some time, space and probably, let's be honest, some tissues. Maybe a delicious snack or a cup of tea, too.

In this exercise, you're going to try to cultivate sympathy – and empathy – for the person who hurt you. To reiterate: this is not about excusing their behaviour. It is not about what they did being okay. It wasn't okay, it wasn't alright, they wronged you, they hurt you and you don't have to be okay with that right now. This is straight-up forgiveness science. You need to reduce the injustice gap so that you can begin to forgive, so that you can move on and so that you can experience the many benefits of forgiveness expressed in the previous chapter.

You want the perpetrator to have suffered, too, so you're going to think about the ways they have suffered. You're going to think, now, about the things that led that person to hurt you: the ways they were wronged and the hurts they have felt. You're going to think of what needs they wanted to be met by their action toward you. These aren't excuses: these are rational, cognitive assessments of what happened.

I know how hard this is. (That's why you've got the tissues, tea and a snack.) I've been there. I am here with you right now. I get it. This is hard and I believe in you.

So ask yourself the following three questions, first posed by the forgiveness researchers at the University of California, Berkeley:

1 What was life like for this person while growing up?

2 What wounds did he or she suffer from others that could have made him or her more likely to hurt you?

3 What kinds of extra pressures or stresses were in this person's life at the time he or she offended you?

Maybe you don't know the actual answers, and that's okay. Make it up. Imagine the reasons that these things *might* have happened. Like I said before, this isn't going to be fact checked: your journal isn't a newspaper. This is just a cognitive way of reducing the injustice gap, and it's also an exercise in love.

What Happened? (II)

Now turn to a new page in your Forgiveness Journal (see page 41). Tell me another story. I want you to use the compassion and love you discovered in the previous exercise to tell me the story of the person who hurt you.

This is an exercise in putting yourself in someone else's shoes. Give yourself a break from feeling like a victim, and let yourself be a detective. What was the person's motive? What did they hope to achieve?

It's useful to remember that most people don't see themselves as bad people Almost nobody wakes up in the morning and thinks, 'I want to be *bad* today'. People can be selfish, thoughtless, lazy, scared, lonely, desperate or angry. People can do terrible things for all kinds of reasons, but almost never for *nothing*. Looking for these reasons can help us to cultivate a kind of meaning around the event: a fuller, richer narrative.

One of the greatest tools at our disposal is understanding that we have the power to change the narrative ourselves: we get to tell whatever story we want about what happened. We get to make that story as big and rich and compassionate as we like. It's up to us.

Take your time. Be as compassionate as you can to others, as well as to yourself. This isn't easy. I'm proud of you.

When you're ready, let's move on.

3

Acknowledgment

There's somebody in your story we need to forgive first, before we can forgive anyone else.

This person is vulnerable. This person is flawed. This person hasn't always done the right thing, or even the good thing. Maybe this person has done terrible things. Maybe this person has made bad choices. Maybe this person has hurt people, or acted in ways that caused others to be hurt. Maybe this person hurt themselves. You know who I mean: I mean you.

Before we can even think of forgiving anybody else, we need to think about forgiving ourselves. We need to understand ourselves and our own part in the story. We need to take a few moments – the length of this chapter, barely a couple of thousand words – to let ourselves be more complex than just pain.

Who Are You? (I)

Come with me. I want you to sketch yourself on a page of your Forgiveness Journal (see page 41). You don't have to be a great artist; a stick figure is fine, although art – creating something out of nothing – is a wonderful way to heal. Don't be afraid to make this journal beautiful. Don't be scared of making something gorgeous out of trauma, something satisfying out of pain. Draw yourself, paint yourself, make a person. Look, it's you!

Write your name above the sketch. Now, set a timer for three minutes. Without thinking too much, write down (around the sketch) words that come to mind to describe you. Adjectives, titles, nouns. Be honest. Be clear. Don't self-edit; nobody will see this except you.

Look at the words you've written. Who are you? How many words are positive? How many are negative? How many are about the pain you suffered? What story are these words telling?

Maybe your words are more
positive than negative, maybe
there's nothing about the pain.
In that case, let's consider whether the
impact of the incident is as great as it used
to be. Did it change your life as much as
you thought it did? Is the injustice gap
(see page 49) as vast as it seemed before?
Be fair. Look at how far you've come and
what you've achieved. Feel that injustice gap
shrinking. Visualize it. Look at all the things
you have. Does the person who hurt you have
these things? Is this how they might feel?

Or maybe it's the other way around. Maybe your
words are more negative than positive. Perhaps your
adjectives are harsh and difficult to swallow. Maybe
you don't like anything about yourself. If that's the
case, the next exercise is for you.

Who Are You? (II)

Turn to a new page in the Forgiveness Journal
(see page 41). You're going to describe yourself like
somebody who loves you would describe you. That
person may be someone you know – a parent, partner,
friend or child – or maybe not. Maybe it's me: a
neutral third party, disposed to think kindly of you
(because you bought my book), looking for all your
best qualities. Or maybe it's you, thinking of yourself
the way you would a trusted friend.

Ask yourself these questions:

- What's your most beautiful feature?

- What's your most attractive personality trait?

- Who trusts you?

- Who do you want to be?

- How would someone who loves you look at you?

This might be really hard for you. And you know what? I don't care. It's not impossible, I promise. You are loveable. You are redeemable. You are loved. You are worthwhile, and this exercise is worthwhile. You are more than just damage. You are more than just pain.

Self-guilt

We are all full, rich, complex characters in need of forgiveness. Late at night, or when we're alone, we're all secretly wondering what we did to deserve the pain we feel. We all have things we hold against ourselves, things we worry about, things we come back to again and again when we're alone and scared. We each have a little voice of self-guilt that wonders:

If only I had….

If only I hadn't …

Why did I …

I can't believe I …

I wish I hadn't …

I wish I had …

I wish …

I want …

Why me?

Why then?

Why now?

What did I do to deserve it?

I want to be clear about one thing, right now: you didn't deserve it. You didn't deserve *any* of it, and it wasn't fair.

You've tried ignoring that little voice of self-guilt. We all have. Maybe you've been told that the pain wasn't your fault. Maybe someone else has tried to explain to you why you didn't deserve it. And still, you wonder. You want to move past the pain but you can't. That voice won't shut up.

So what if we tried confronting that stubborn inner voice? What if we were to say, 'Fine. I did what I had to do. I know what I did, and it got me here. It got me *out*, to this place where I can begin to forgive. And that's incredible.'

While the previous chapter was all about why the person who hurt us did what *they* did, this chapter focuses on why *we* did what *we* did. Because we had choices, too. We aren't powerless. We are strong and capable and brave. We've made choices. We've done things. We are more than what was done to us. This chapter is about reclaiming ourselves, in all our flawed and broken glory; it's about our beautiful, rich, damaged selves.

Forgiving Yourself

Before we address this question, let's bring our Forgiveness Journals (see page 41) to the table, and maybe make ourselves a cup of tea and snack again, too. Why not? This is *all* very hard.

Take a moment, now, to really examine your initial story (see Exercise: What Happened (I), page 42). Are there places you've blamed yourself? Is that blame fair? Would you blame a friend or a sibling for something similar? Can you forgive yourself for those things? Can you forgive yourself for anything you did that you feel contributed to the trauma?

Now (and yes, this just gets more and more meta), can you forgive yourself for any victim-blaming you've internalized or had thrust upon you? Can you forgive the ways you've treated yourself in the past? Can you forgive the thoughts you've had that hurt you? You have to forgive the hurt that you've done yourself, too. You have to forgive the times you've believed this was your fault. Forgive yourself for failing to forgive yourself.

Finally, can you forgive yourself for having the audacity to want to move on? Can you forgive yourself your need for a future? Can you forgive yourself the self-indulgence of raking back through the past, of opening all those boxes of hidden pain, of trying to become more?

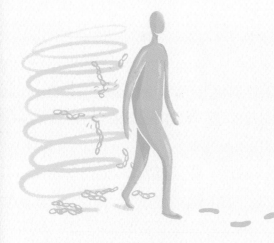

EXERCISE

What Happened? (III)

Turn to a fresh page in the Forgiveness Journal
(see page 41). This time I want a bigger story. I want
a story that's about you.

I don't want to hear anything much about the person
who hurt you. This is *your* story, not theirs. This is about
what *you* did. In fact, I want you to leave them out of it
entirely. I want this story to be full of the pronoun 'I'.
Make it a first-person account of everything you did.
Give me active verbs. Give me choices. The only 'doing
words' in this story should be done by you. I'm not
interested in the other person. They're boring to me.
You're the one we care about here. This is your story.
It's you who matters. I want you to tell me what
happened before, and what happened after.

This isn't a story about things being done to you. This
is a story about things you did. This is the story of you.

Well done. I'm proud of you. This chapter hasn't been
easy – none of this is easy – but it's worth it.

4

Meaning

We can't go back and undo the past. We can't change the hurt we suffered but we can rejoice in the person we've become due to that hurt. For instance, we can appreciate the incredible compassion or patience we've learned to cultivate. We can learn from the things that have happened to us. There can be a purpose to resentment, a purpose to pain, a purpose to suffering.

Often, the aftermath of our own pain makes us more empathetic to the pain of other people; it makes us kinder and more compassionate, reminding us that everyone in life is going through their own private struggles. I know this is true of you because you're the kind of brilliant, compassionate, thoughtful person who wants to try and forgive enough that you're already most of the way through this book.

This is a hard book! The
set of exercises you've
worked through have
been complicated, difficult
and emotionally traumatizing,
and yet somehow you've kept on
reading. Because that's the person
you are: you're determined and
brave and kind. You're *you*.

Gratitude

It's not possible to fake forgiveness; faking it 'til we make it just won't work in this instance. As we discovered in Chapter 2 (see page 45), we can decide to forgive, but unless we really *feel* it, we'll still suffer the detrimental effects of 'unforgiveness'.

What does work is gratitude. You can learn to love the life you have. You can learn to notice the things that you love. You can learn to love more things. You can learn to be happier. Learning all these things helps to reduces stress, which, as you'll recall from previous chapters, increases our physical health.

Studies have shown that people who write about the things in life for which they are grateful report significantly improved mental health, on an ongoing basis.[7] Even after the studies ended, and participants stopped writing, they *still* reported feeling better, because they had trained their brains to look for the good. They also slept better, were in less pain, were less anxious and less depressed.

We have to teach ourselves to focus on what we have, not what we don't have (what remains, not what was taken). We have to train ourselves to focus on the positive and the things we have. The way we do this (you guessed it) is by writing.

We've talked a lot about the benefits of writing and now, rather than using it to process trauma, we're going to use it to focus on the positive. We're going to specifically describe good things in our life, with as much loving detail and precision as possible.

Professor Robert Emmons, the world's leading scholar of gratitude studies, believes that the main benefits of gratitude journals come from being really specific about the things we like.[8] Say, for example, you're grateful for the mug of tea in front of you. Why do you love this mug in particular? Why this brand of tea? Why the kettle? Why are you glad to have this tea right this minute?

Gratitude Journal

Every night, at the same time before you sleep, you're
going to take your Forgiveness Journal (see page 41)
and write three things about the day that you're
grateful for. Do this every day for six weeks at least,
although you might find it's a good habit to stick with!

You can use the sample template opposite or make up
your own.

Date ....

I'm grateful today for [*the name of person*], who.................

....

....

....

....

I'm grateful today for [*a little thing that improved your life*] because...

....

....

....

....

I'm grateful today for [*a life circumstance, such as health, wealth, weather, family or friends*] ....

....

....

....

....

Enough is Enough

We have everything we're grateful for because of who we are, and we are who we are because of everything that has happened to us.

The ways we've been hurt have shaped us. We've shaped our experiences. We can't change the past, nor can we change other people, but we can change the way we live and the way we think. We have agency. We make our own choices. We go forward carrying everything we've been given. We are resourceful creatures, putting everything to use, including pain. Pain shapes us and makes us, and we make our lives.

I don't, myself, believe in destiny. Maybe you do. Many people believe that pain helps us to become the person who can fulfil our fate. Personally, I think pain simply makes us who we are. Without pain we would have been somebody different, somebody who made different choices, somebody who wasn't reading – or writing – this book right now.

In lots of ways, this book is about writing as connection. You've written your story and I've been writing to you. We've connected and we are healing.

You don't get a second go in life, and wishing you could won't change anything. It will only make the present harder to bear, and life is hard enough as it is. You know that. You, of all people, know that. You've suffered enough, don't you think?

Body Scan (II)

Remember the body scan exercise from the beginning of this book? I want you to turn back to that page (see page 33), and give it another go.

Close your eyes and breathe evenly: breathe in for a count of four, breathe out for a count of four. Push the breath right out of you, then haul it right back in.

I want you to do something a little different this time. I want you to focus on everything you're capable of. Not your pain, or not solely your pain. I want you to notice your brilliant, magnificent, capable body.

Breathe in and breathe out. Bring the air (whatever this looks like for you) right down to your toes. Feel the air through your whole body: the spine, the belly, the hips, the legs, the four corners of the feet. Remember? Feel your toes. Feel every toe on each foot. Thank each toe for your balance, stability, even elegance. Thank each toe for whatever you can, whatever applies to you. I know this seems silly but try it. Breathe in that gratitude. Breathe out that pain.

Breathe for the balls of your feet, the soles of your feet, the tops of your feet. Thank your feet. Breathe for your legs. Breathe all the way up your femurs, tibia and fibia. Breathe for your bones and muscles. Think of everything your legs give you. Maybe it's running or standing or walking. Maybe it's looking good in a pair of jeans. Breathe that generosity and gratitude for your legs right down.

Breathe for your thighs, hips and pelvis. Bring the attention and the air right down into your organs and blood. Bring your attention and your gratitude there. You have a body. It is a brilliant body, just as it is. Every part of you is good, just as it is, even the damaged parts, even the wounded parts. Pain is a message that prompts us to rest, just as fever is a signal that the body is fighting a battle. Thank you, clever body.

Move your attention to your spine, your rib cage, your lower back, your upper back, your belly, your chest and your shoulders. Gratitude in, pain out.

Now bring your attention to your arms, elbows, hands and fingers. Your fingertips, palms and wrists, too. Let your attention run along the lines of the bones, and then back up into the shoulders, the top of your spine, the base of your neck, your throat, your chin, your smile, your nose and your eyes. Thank you, senses. Gratitude in, as deep and powerful and silly as you can.

Pain out. Gratitude in.

Feel the world around you and think gratitude for that,
too. Think gratitude for the room you're sitting in and
the wide world outside. Think gratitude for this
moment of peace. Think gratitude even for the pain
that brought you here. That pain got you to this quiet
moment, where you are good enough. Know that.
Know that you're good enough.

5

Perspective
and
Gratitude

'What matters in life is not what happens to you but what you remember and how you remember it,' wrote Gabriel García Márquez.[9]

Working through this book has been a series of rememberings and rewritings: a series of meanings. We've been reclaiming our agency, and finding ourselves as complete people.

Each time we tell a version of our story it becomes richer and more interesting. Every time we tell it, we move away from the narrative that's been crushing us. Every time we tell it a different way, we find new meanings, new perspectives and new ways to communicate our needs and wants, our histories and desires.

Reclaiming Your Story

In this final chapter, we're going to try to bring the three versions of our stories together: the story of our pain, the story of the other person's pain and choices and the story of our choices. We're going to take those stories and make something. We're going to use those stories to make a *meaning*. We are going to find meaning here. We're going to see how what happened changed us – how it changed the world.

This chapter is also about empathy, of course. It's about understanding that what happened to us also happened to the person who hurt us. It's about decentralizing the pain we feel and making it part of a broader narrative. It's about making a whole story around us. It's about perspective, gratitude and meaning.

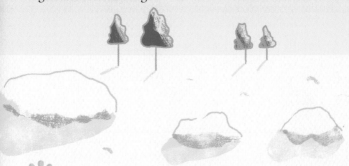

The secret, you see, is making it look like you meant to do it all along. Think: feature not bug. Think, even if you don't believe it, that everything happens for a reason, and you (brilliant, complicated, thoughtful you!) are the reason. You make the reason.

I'm not saying that I want you to believe those terrible things happened because you deserved them or that they were in some way preordained. I don't believe, and I don't want you to believe, that things would have been worse if the terrible things had never happened. The world isn't a better place because you suffered; it's simply *the* place. This is all there is – and it is beautiful.

Perspective and Gratitude

Write a Letter to the Person Who Hurt You

We're going to move on, now, from expressive writing to transactional writing. Expressive writing is a tool for self-reflection that uses the act of writing to explore our deepest thoughts and emotions, whereas transactional writing offers an exchange of information. For this exercise, we're going to write to the person who hurt us and tell them what we've learned.

Don't worry, we're not going to send this letter to the person – at least, not unless you really want to, and even then I'd advise you to hang on to it for a few weeks to see if you still feel the same.

I want you to write to this person formally, telling them what you've learned. Tell them the story you've made from the retellings and re-rememberings. Tell them who you've become, who you are and how you got here. Say everything you have always wanted to say to them. You are powerful and you are merciful. You are in charge, here, not them. This is *your* moment. As Gandhi said, 'The weak can never forgive. Forgiveness is the attribute of the strong.' You are so strong.

Tell this person what you know now about why they acted the way they did. Tell them the ways they hurt you. Use all the stories you've written in your

Forgiveness Journal (see page 41) to guide you. Use all your anger and pain, all your love and compassion, all your agency and wisdom. You are the person writing the letter. You are the person in charge. Tell them what they did. Tell them why it was wrong. And tell them, at last, that you forgive them. That you are free of them, free of what happened.

This letter isn't intended to make the person who hurt you feel guilt, of course. It's not intended to make them feel bad. It's intended to make *you* feel good. This is a gift you're giving another human being because you can. You have power, you have agency, you have choice.

Visualize Meeting the Person

Some researchers suggest that when you reach this stage in the forgiveness process you should reach out to this person in real life – a phone call, a kind word – but there's one more thing I think we should try before we get there. One last thing to do.

Visualize somewhere you feel completely safe and secure. Somewhere you feel in charge, confident and capable. Somewhere you feel brave and loved. (I'm picturing my sitting room, and you can, too, if you want: there's a big mustard-yellow armchair, soft blankets, a tall bookcase, a sofa. It's a safe room, a soft room, a room with a door.)

Imagine there's a knock at the door. It's the person who hurt you and they want to come in. (Don't worry. They can't hurt you again. They know this is a safe place. You can make them leave any time.) Invite them in, if you can. Picture them perched awkwardly on the edge of a chair, looking at how well you've done to have this safe place. Picture them knowing how well you've done altogether. Look them in the eye, if you can.

Say everything you want to say. Say everything you wrote in your letter (see page 88) — every feeling, every moment, every consequence. And then say, out loud, in your own words (or mine), something like, 'I forgive you. You can go.'

Tell this person, or rather, this manifestation of the person, to go. Tell this person who you have resented and unforgiven for so long, 'You can go. You have to go. I want you to go.'

I want you to be free of this person, free of your resentment toward this person, so that, if you want, and if it's applicable, you can work on rebuilding the relationship. You can, if you like, reach out to this person freely and of your own volition. You don't have to carry this ghost with whom you've been angry for so long. You can meet them person to person, if that's what you want. You can start again.

Moving on with Your Life

This is how we end the story that began in pain: you sitting quietly, peacefully writing. You, with your cup of tea, and your pen, and your journal full of thoughts and stories.

This is the moment we've been waiting for, the moment when the story is over, and a new one can begin. This is the moment when you can close this book and choose another from the shelf. Choose a new story.

Endnotes

1   Aldwin, Carolyn, 'Best To Not Sweat The Small Stuff, Because It Could Kill You', *NPR*, 2014, https://www.npr.org/transcripts/349875448.

2   Nerurkar, Adita, Bitton, Asaf, Davis, Roger B., Phillips, Russell S. & Yeh, Gloria, 'When Physicians Counsel About Stress: Results of a National Study', *JAMA Intern Med.*, 2013, 173(1), 76–77, DOI:10.1001/2013.jamainternmed.480.

3   Baikie, Karen, & Wilhelm, Kay, 'Emotional and physical health benefits of expressive writing', *Advances in Psychiatric Treatment*, 2005, 11(5), 338–346, DOI:10.1192/apt.11.5.338.

4   Robinson, Hayley, Jarrett, Paul & Vedhara, Kavita & Broadbent, Elizabeth, 'The effects of expressive writing before or after punch biopsy on wound healing'. *Brain, Behavior, and Immunity*, 2016, 61, 217–227, DOI: 10.1016/j.bbi.2016.11.025.

5   Worthington, Everett L. Jr. & Scherer, Michael, 'Forgiveness is an emotion focused coping strategy that can reduce health risks and promote health resilience: theory, review, and hypotheses', *Psychology & Health*, 2004, 19(3), 385–405.

6   Davis, Don, Yang, Xioahui, DeBlaere, Cirleen, McElroy, Stacey E., Van Tongeren, Daryl R., Hook, Joshua N. & Worthington, Everett L. Jnr., 'The Injustice Gap', *Psychology of Religion and Spirituality*, 2016, 8(3), 175–184, DOI: 10.1037/rel0000042.

7 Wong, Joel Y., Owen, Jesse, Gabana, Nicole T., Brown, Joshua W., McInnis, Sydney, Toth, Paul & Gilman, Lynn, 'Does gratitude writing improve the mental health of psychotherapy clients? Evidence from a randomized controlled trial', *Psychotherapy Research*, 2018, 28(2), 192–202, DOI: 10.1080/10503307.2016.1169332.

8 Emmons, Robert A., *Gratitude Works!*. (San Francisco: Jossey-Bass, 2013)

9 García Márquez, Gabriel, *Living to Tell the Tale*. (London: Penguin Books, 2014)